# HORN
# BIG BOOK of DISNEY SONGS

## Available for
FLUTE, CLARINET, ALTO SAX, TENOR SAX, TRUMPET, HORN, TROMBONE, VIOLIN, VIOLA, CELLO

Note: The keys in this book do not match the other wind instruments.

ISBN 978-1-4584-1136-5

**Walt Disney Music Company**
**Wonderland Music Company, Inc.**

DISTRIBUTED BY

**HAL•LEONARD®**
CORPORATION

7777 W. BLUEMOUND RD. P.O. BOX 13819 MILWAUKEE, WI 53213

In Australia Contact:
Hal Leonard Australia Pty. Ltd.
4 Lentara Court
Cheltenham, Victoria, 3192 Australia
Email: ausadmin@halleonard.com.au

Visit Hal Leonard Online at
**www.halleonard.com**

# CONTENTS

# ALICE IN WONDERLAND

from Walt Disney's ALICE IN WONDERLAND

**Horn**

Words by BOB HILLIARD
Music by SAMMY FAIN

# THE BALLAD OF DAVY CROCKETT

from Walt Disney's DAVY CROCKETT

Words by TOM BLACKBURN
Music by GEORGE BRUNS

# BE OUR GUEST
from Walt Disney's BEAUTY AND THE BEAST

Lyrics by HOWARD ASHMAN
Music by ALAN MENKEN

# THE BARE NECESSITIES

from Walt Disney's THE JUNGLE BOOK

HORN

Words and Music by
TERRY GILKYSON

# BEAUTY AND THE BEAST

from Walt Disney's BEAUTY AND THE BEAST

Horn

Lyrics by HOWARD ASHMAN
Music by ALAN MENKEN

# BELLA NOTTE
## (This Is the Night)
from Walt Disney's LADY AND THE TRAMP

HORN

Words and Music by PEGGY LEE
and SONNY BURKE

# BIBBIDI-BOBBIDI-BOO
## (The Magic Song)
from Walt Disney's CINDERELLA

Words by JERRY LIVINGSTON
Music by MACK DAVID and AL HOFFMAN

# CRUELLA DE VIL
from Walt Disney's 101 DALMATIANS

Words and Music by
MEL LEVEN

**Slow Blues**

# BREAKING FREE

from the Disney Channel Original Movie HIGH SCHOOL MUSICAL

HORN

Words and Music by
JAMIE HOUSTON

**Moderately**

# BEST OF FRIENDS

from Walt Disney's THE FOX AND THE HOUND

**HORN**

Words by STAN FIDEL
Music by RICHARD JOHNSTON

**Moderately**

# CAN YOU FEEL THE LOVE TONIGHT

from Walt Disney Pictures' THE LION KING

HORN

Music by ELTON JOHN
Lyrics by TIM RICE

**Pop Ballad**

# CANDLE ON THE WATER

from Walt Disney's PETE'S DRAGON

**Horn**

Words and Music by AL KASHA
and JOEL HIRSCHHORN

# CHIM CHIM CHER-EE

from Walt Disney's MARY POPPINS

Horn

Words and Music by RICHARD M. SHERMAN
and ROBERT B. SHERMAN

# COLORS OF THE WIND

from Walt Disney's POCAHONTAS

HORN

Music by ALAN MENKEN
Lyrics by STEPHEN SCHWARTZ

# A DREAM IS A WISH YOUR HEART MAKES

from Walt Disney's CINDERELLA

Words and Music by MACK DAVID,
AL HOFFMAN and JERRY LIVINGSTON

# CIRCLE OF LIFE

from Walt Disney Pictures' THE LION KING

**HORN**

Music by ELTON JOHN
Lyrics by TIM RICE

**Moderately (with an African beat)**

# GO THE DISTANCE

from Walt Disney Pictures' HERCULES

HORN

Music by ALAN MENKEN
Lyrics by DAVID ZIPPEL

# FRIEND LIKE ME

from Walt Disney's ALADDIN

Horn

Lyrics by HOWARD ASHMAN
Music by ALAN MENKEN

# GOD HELP THE OUTCASTS

from Walt Disney's THE HUNCHBACK OF NOTRE DAME

Horn

Music by ALAN MENKEN
Lyrics by STEPHEN SCHWARTZ

# HOW D'YE DO AND SHAKE HANDS
from Walt Disney's ALICE IN WONDERLAND

Words by CY COBEN
Music by OLIVER WALLACE

# HAKUNA MATATA

from Walt Disney Pictures' THE LION KING

HORN

Music by ELTON JOHN
Lyrics by TIM RICE

# HE'S A TRAMP
from Walt Disney's LADY AND THE TRAMP

Words and Music by PEGGY LEE
and SONNY BURKE

**Moderately**

# I JUST CAN'T WAIT TO BE KING

from Walt Disney Pictures' THE LION KING

Horn

Music by ELTON JOHN
Lyrics by TIM RICE

# I'M LATE
from Walt Disney's ALICE IN WONDERLAND

Words by BOB HILLIARD
Music by SAMMY FAIN

# IF I NEVER KNEW YOU

## (Love Theme from POCAHONTAS)
### from Walt Disney's POCAHONTAS

HORN

Music by ALAN MENKEN
Lyrics by STEPHEN SCHWARTZ

# IT'S A SMALL WORLD

from Disneyland Resort® and Magic Kingdom® Park

HORN

Words and Music by RICHARD M. SHERMAN
and ROBERT B. SHERMAN

# LAVENDER BLUE

(Dilly Dilly)

from Walt Disney's SO DEAR TO MY HEART

Words by LARRY MOREY
Music by ELIOT DANIEL

# LET'S GET TOGETHER

from Walt Disney Pictures' THE PARENT TRAP

© 1960 Wonderland Music Company, Inc.
Copyright Renewed

Words and Music by RICHARD M. SHERMAN
and ROBERT B. SHERMAN

# LET'S GO FLY A KITE

from Walt Disney's MARY POPPINS

**Horn**

Words and Music by RICHARD M. SHERMAN
and ROBERT B. SHERMAN

# MY FUNNY FRIEND AND ME

from Walt Disney Pictures' THE EMPEROR'S NEW GROOVE

Lyrics by STING
Music by STING and DAVID HARTLEY

# LITTLE APRIL SHOWER
from Walt Disney's BAMBI

Horn

Words by LARRY MOREY
Music by FRANK CHURCHILL

# THE LORD IS GOOD TO ME
from Walt Disney's MELODY TIME
from Walt Disney's JOHNNY APPLESEED

Words and Music by KIM GANNON
and WALTER KENT

# MICKEY MOUSE MARCH

from Walt Disney's THE MICKEY MOUSE CLUB

Words and Music by
JIMMIE DODD

# KISS THE GIRL

from Walt Disney's THE LITTLE MERMAID

Horn

Music by ALAN MENKEN
Lyrics by HOWARD ASHMAN

# NEVER SMILE AT A CROCODILE

from Walt Disney's PETER PAN

Horn

Words by JACK LAWRENCE
Music by FRANK CHURCHILL

# PART OF YOUR WORLD

from Walt Disney's THE LITTLE MERMAID

HORN

Music by ALAN MENKEN
Lyrics by HOWARD ASHMAN

# ONCE UPON A DREAM
from Walt Disney's SLEEPING BEAUTY

HORN

Words and Music by SAMMY FAIN
and JACK LAWRENCE
Adapted from a Theme by Tchaikovsky

# REFLECTION
from Walt Disney Pictures' MULAN

Music by MATTHEW WILDER
Lyrics by DAVID ZIPPEL

# A PIRATE'S LIFE

from Walt Disney's PETER PAN

Horn

Words by ED PENNER
Music by OLIVER WALLACE

**Moderately, with a bounce**

# SCALES AND ARPEGGIOS

from Walt Disney's THE ARISTOCATS

Words and Music by RICHARD M. SHERMAN
and ROBERT B. SHERMAN

**Moderately**

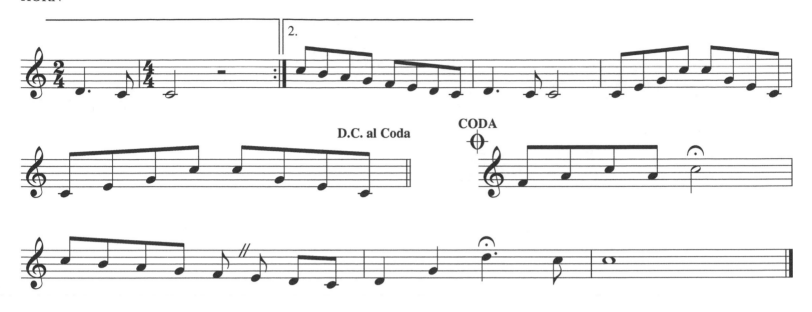

# THE SECOND STAR TO THE RIGHT

from Walt Disney's PETER PAN

Words by SAMMY CAHN
Music by SAMMY FAIN

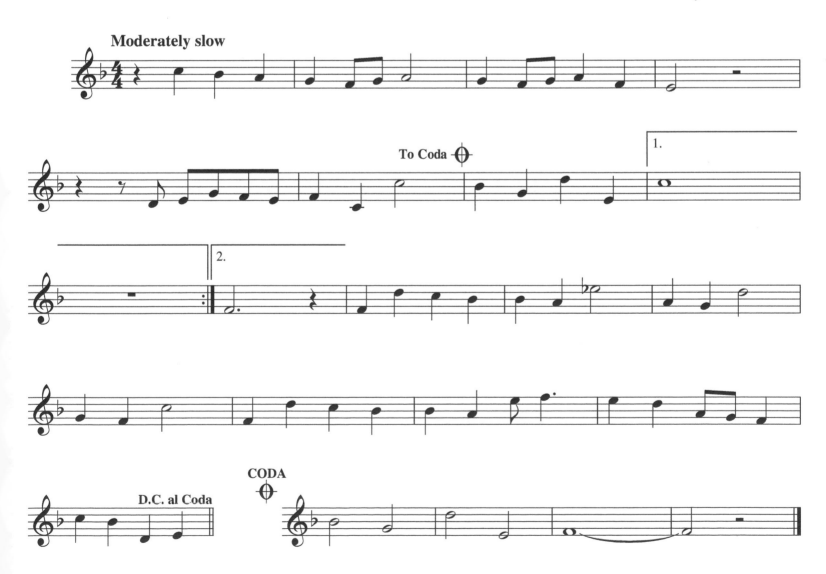

# SALUDOS AMIGOS

from Walt Disney's SALUDOS AMIGOS
from Walt Disney's THE THREE CABALLEROS

HORN

Words by NED WASHINGTON
Music by CHARLES WOLCOTT

**With spirit**

# SO THIS IS LOVE
## (The Cinderella Waltz)
from Walt Disney's CINDERELLA

HORN

Words and Music by MACK DAVID,
AL HOFFMAN and JERRY LIVINGSTON

# THE SIAMESE CAT SONG

from Walt Disney's LADY AND THE TRAMP

Horn

Words and Music by PEGGY LEE
and SONNY BURKE

# SOONER OR LATER

from Walt Disney's SONG OF THE SOUTH

Words and Music by RAY GILBERT
and CHARLES WOLCOTT

(knock, knock)

(knock, knock)

1.

2.

# SOMEDAY

Horn

from Walt Disney's THE HUNCHBACK OF NOTRE DAME

Music by ALAN MENKEN
Lyrics by STEPHEN SCHWARTZ

# SOMEONE'S WAITING FOR YOU

from Walt Disney's THE RESCUERS

HORN

Words by CAROL CONNORS and AYN ROBBINS
Music by SAMMY FAIN

# A SPOONFUL OF SUGAR

from Walt Disney's MARY POPPINS

Horn

Words and Music by RICHARD M. SHERMAN
and ROBERT B. SHERMAN

# THESE ARE THE BEST TIMES

from Walt Disney Productions' SUPERDAD

HORN

Words and Music by
SHANE TATUM

# SWEET SURRENDER

from Walt Disney's THE BEARS AND I

Horn

Words and Music by
JOHN DENVER

# TOYLAND MARCH
from Walt Disney's BABES IN TOYLAND

Adapted from V. HERBERT Melody
Words by MEL LEVEN
Music by GEORGE BRUNS

**March tempo**

# TRASHIN' THE CAMP

from Walt Disney Pictures' TARZAN™

**HORN**

Words and Music by
PHIL COLLINS

*Wooh!* *Wooh!*

*Wooh!* *Wooh!* *Wooh!*

# WESTWARD HO, THE WAGONS!

from Walt Disney's WESTWARD HO, THE WAGONS!

Words by TOM BLACKBURN
Music by GEORGE BRUNS

# SUPERCALIFRAGILISTICEXPIALIDOCIOUS

from Walt Disney's MARY POPPINS

HORN

Words and Music by RICHARD M. SHERMAN
and ROBERT B. SHERMAN

**Brightly**

# THE UNBIRTHDAY SONG

from Walt Disney's ALICE IN WONDERLAND

**Horn**

Words and Music by MACK DAVID,
AL HOFFMAN and JERRY LIVINGSTON

# UNDER THE SEA

from Walt Disney's THE LITTLE MERMAID

Horn

Music by ALAN MENKEN
Lyrics by HOWARD ASHMAN

# WE'RE ALL IN THIS TOGETHER

from the Disney Channel Original Movie HIGH SCHOOL MUSICAL

HORN

Words and Music by MATTHEW GERRARD
and ROBBIE NEVIL

# WHEN SHE LOVED ME

from Walt Disney Pictures' TOY STORY 2 - A Pixar Film

HORN

Music and Lyrics by
RANDY NEWMAN

**Tenderly, very freely**

# WINNIE THE POOH
from Walt Disney's THE MANY ADVENTURES OF WINNIE THE POOH

Words and Music by RICHARD M. SHERMAN
and ROBERT B. SHERMAN

**Tenderly**

# WHERE THE DREAM TAKES YOU

from Walt Disney Pictures' ATLANTIS: THE LOST EMPIRE

HORN

Lyrics by DIANE WARREN
Music by DIANE WARREN
and JAMES NEWTON HOWARD

# A WHOLE NEW WORLD

from Walt Disney's ALADDIN

HORN

Music by ALAN MENKEN
Lyrics by TIM RICE

# A WHALE OF A TALE
from Walt Disney's 20,000 LEAGUES UNDER THE SEA

Horn

Words and Music by NORMAN GIMBEL
and AL HOFFMAN

# THE WONDERFUL THING ABOUT TIGGERS
from Walt Disney's THE MANY ADVENTURES OF WINNIE THE POOH

Words and Music by RICHARD M. SHERMAN
and ROBERT B. SHERMAN

# YO HO
## (A Pirate's Life for Me)
from PIRATES OF THE CARIBBEAN at Disneyland Park and Magic Kingdom Park

Words by XAVIER ATENCIO
Music by GEORGE BRUNS

# WRINGLE WRANGLE
## (A Pretty Woman's Love)
from Walt Disney's WESTWARD HO, THE WAGONS!

HORN

Words and Music by
STAN JONES

# WRITTEN IN THE STARS

from Elton John and Tim Rice's AIDA

HORN

Music by ELTON JOHN
Lyrics by TIM RICE

# YOU ARE THE MUSIC IN ME

from the Disney Channel Original Movie HIGH SCHOOL MUSICAL 2

HORN

Words and Music by
JAMIE HOUSTON

Moderately fast Rock

# YOU'LL BE IN MY HEART

(Pop Version)

from Walt Disney Pictures' TARZAN™

**HORN**

Words and Music by
PHIL COLLINS

# YOU CAN FLY! YOU CAN FLY! YOU CAN FLY!

HORN

from Walt Disney's PETER PAN

Words by SAMMY CAHN
Music by SAMMY FAIN

# YOU'VE GOT A FRIEND IN ME

from Walt Disney's TOY STORY

HORN

Music and Lyrics by
RANDY NEWMAN

# ZERO TO HERO

from Walt Disney Pictures' HERCULES

HORN

Music by ALAN MENKEN
Lyrics by DAVID ZIPPEL

# ZIP-A-DEE-DOO-DAH

from Walt Disney's SONG OF THE SOUTH

HORN

Words by RAY GILBERT
Music by ALLIE WRUBEL